ISBN: 979-8-9856174-3-6
PAPERBACK

Printed in the United States of American

First edition: 2022
First printing 2022

Noreen Jordan is a licensed Mental Health Professional, Christian Counselor, Speaker, Author, Trainer, and Consultant specializing in working with individuals, couples, families, and corporations who have experienced trauma and/ or have witnessed traumatic events. She has also worked with first responders and military personnel, both nationally and internationally. She is the president/CEO of her own business along with a non-profit organization.

Noreen empowers individuals and couples to overcome personal obstacles so that they can once again live purposefully and joy-filled lives while honoring their past and living in the present and for the future.

Having overcome her own life-altering trauma, she has the passion to reach out to others and support them in addressing their traumatic experiences. Noreen's own life is living proof of one's ability to overcome life's obstacles, and she is determined to help others to reclaim their Purpose, Power, and Confidence.

She has her Master of Arts in Marital and Family Therapy from Azusa Pacific University and is a Licensed Professional Counselor.
She is a Certified Trauma Professional and Critical Incident Stress Debriefer/Manager (CISD/CISM) and has over 20+ years of Counseling, Consulting Training, and Behavioral health experience in a variety of settings. It is by God's grace that she is an overcomer.

Welcome & Thank You!

Congratulations!
Self-Care is important and you have taken a step forward by purchasing this journal.
I commend you for understanding how important your well-being is.
You have made yourself a priority.
Doing so not only benefits you, but the people you love as well.
The people who love you and depend on you would much rather see you positive, full of energy and happy, than tired and unhappy.

This Journal will help to equip you with the tools to make self-care an ongoing part of your life's journey.

Thank you for choosing our journal to assist you in your journey.

This Journal Belongs to:

_____

Prayer Journal

Date ....

Prayers

Daily Verse & Inspiration

Praises & Gratitude

Thoughts

Prayer Journal

Date ....

Prayers

Daily Verse & Inspiration

Praises & Gratitude

Thoughts

Prayer Journal

Date ....

Prayers

┌───┐
│   *Daily Verse & Inspiration*   │
│   │
│   │
└───┘

Praises & Gratitude

Thoughts

Prayer Journal

Date ....

Prayers

Daily Verse & Inspiration

Praises & Gratitude

Thoughts

Prayer Journal

Date ....

Prayers

Daily Verse & Inspiration

Praises & Gratitude

Thoughts

Prayer Journal

Date ....

Prayers

Daily Verse & Inspiration

Praises & Gratitude

Thoughts

Prayer Journal

Date ....

Prayers

Daily Verse & Inspiration

Praises & Gratitude

Thoughts

Prayer Journal

Date ....

Prayers

Daily Verse & Inspiration

Praises & Gratitude

Thoughts

Prayer Journal

Date ....

Prayers

Daily Verse & Inspiration

Praises & Gratitude

Thoughts

Prayer Journal

Date ....

Prayers

Daily Verse & Inspiration

Praises & Gratitude

Thoughts

Prayer Journal

Date ....

Prayers

Daily Verse & Inspiration

Praises & Gratitude

Thoughts

Prayer Journal

Date ....

Prayers

Daily Verse & Inspiration

Praises & Gratitude

Thoughts

Prayer Journal

Date _____

Prayers

Daily Verse & Inspiration

Praises & Gratitude

Thoughts

Prayer Journal

Date ....

Prayers

Daily Verse & Inspiration

Praises & Gratitude

Thoughts

Prayer Journal

Date

 *Prayers*

Daily Verse & Inspiration

Praises & Gratitude

Thoughts

Prayer Journal

Date ....

Prayers

_____

_____

_____

Daily Verse & Inspiration

Praises & Gratitude

Thoughts

Prayer Journal

Date _____

Prayers

Daily Verse & Inspiration

Praises & Gratitude

Thoughts

Prayer Journal

Date ....

Prayers

Daily Verse & Inspiration

Praises & Gratitude

Thoughts

Prayer Journal

Date _____

Prayers

Daily Verse & Inspiration

Praises & Gratitude

Thoughts

Prayer Journal

Date ....

Prayers

Daily Verse & Inspiration

Praises & Gratitude

Thoughts

Prayer Journal

Date ....

Prayers

Daily Verse & Inspiration

Praises & Gratitude

Thoughts

Prayer Journal

Date ....

Prayers

....

....

....

Daily Verse & Inspiration

Praises & Gratitude

Thoughts

Prayer Journal

Date _____

Prayers

_____
_____
_____
_____
_____
_____
_____

Daily Verse & Inspiration

Praises & Gratitude

_____
_____

Thoughts

Prayer Journal

Date ....

Prayers

Daily Verse & Inspiration

Praises & Gratitude

Thoughts

Prayer Journal

Date ....

Prayers

Daily Verse & Inspiration

Praises & Gratitude

Thoughts

Prayer Journal

Date ....

Prayers

....

....

....

Daily Verse & Inspiration

Praises & Gratitude

Thoughts

Prayer Journal

Date _____

Prayers

_____
_____
_____
_____
_____
_____
_____

Daily Verse & Inspiration

Praises & Gratitude

_____
_____
_____

Thoughts

Prayer Journal

Date ....

 *Prayers*

....

....

....

Daily Verse & Inspiration

Praises & Gratitude

Thoughts

Prayer Journal

Date ....

Prayers

Daily Verse & Inspiration

Praises & Gratitude

Thoughts

Prayer Journal

Date ....

Prayers

Daily Verse & Inspiration

Praises & Gratitude

Thoughts

Prayer Journal

Date ....

Prayers

Daily Verse & Inspiration

Praises & Gratitude

Thoughts

Prayer Journal

Date ....

Prayers

Daily Verse & Inspiration

Praises & Gratitude

Thoughts

Prayer Journal

Date ....

Prayers

Daily Verse & Inspiration

Praises & Gratitude

Thoughts

Prayer Journal

Date ....

Prayers

....

....

....

Daily Verse & Inspiration

Praises & Gratitude

Thoughts

Prayer Journal

Date ....

Prayers

Daily Verse & Inspiration

Praises & Gratitude

Thoughts

Prayer Journal

Date ....

Prayers

Daily Verse & Inspiration

Praises & Gratitude

Thoughts

Prayer Journal

Date _____

Prayers

Daily Verse & Inspiration

Praises & Gratitude

Thoughts

Prayer Journal

Date ....

Prayers

Daily Verse & Inspiration

Praises & Gratitude

Thoughts

Prayer Journal

Date ....

Prayers

Daily Verse & Inspiration

Praises & Gratitude

Thoughts

Prayer Journal

Date ....

Prayers

Daily Verse & Inspiration

Praises & Gratitude

Thoughts

Prayer Journal

Date ....

Prayers

Daily Verse & Inspiration

Praises & Gratitude

Thoughts

Prayer Journal

Date ....

Prayers

Daily Verse & Inspiration

Praises & Gratitude

Thoughts

Prayer Journal

Date _____

Prayers

Daily Verse & Inspiration

Praises & Gratitude

Thoughts

Prayer Journal

Date _____

Prayers

Daily Verse & Inspiration

Praises & Gratitude

Thoughts

Prayer Journal

Date ....

Prayers

Daily Verse & Inspiration

Praises & Gratitude

Thoughts

Prayer Journal

Date ....

Prayers

Daily Verse & Inspiration

Praises & Gratitude

Thoughts

Prayer Journal

Date _____

Prayers

_____

_____

_____

_____

_____

Daily Verse & Inspiration

Praises & Gratitude

_____

_____

Thoughts

Prayer Journal

Date

Prayers

Daily Verse & Inspiration

Praises & Gratitude

Thoughts

Prayer Journal

Date ....

Prayers

Daily Verse & Inspiration

Praises & Gratitude

Thoughts

Prayer Journal

Date ....

Prayers

Daily Verse & Inspiration

Praises & Gratitude

Thoughts

Prayer Journal

Date _____

Prayers

Daily Verse & Inspiration

Praises & Gratitude

Thoughts

Prayer Journal

Date ....

Prayers

Daily Verse & Inspiration

Praises & Gratitude

Thoughts

Prayer Journal

Date ....

 *Prayers*

Daily Verse & Inspiration

Praises & Gratitude

Thoughts

Prayer Journal

Date ....

Prayers

Daily Verse & Inspiration

Praises & Gratitude

Thoughts

Prayer Journal

Date _____

Prayers

Daily Verse & Inspiration

Praises & Gratitude

Thoughts

Prayer Journal

Date ....

Prayers

Daily Verse & Inspiration

Praises & Gratitude

Thoughts

Prayer Journal

Date _____

 Prayers

Daily Verse & Inspiration

Praises & Gratitude

Thoughts

Prayer Journal

Date ....

Prayers

....

....

....

Daily Verse & Inspiration

Praises & Gratitude

Thoughts

Prayer Journal

Date ....

 *Prayers*

Daily Verse & Inspiration

Praises & Gratitude

Thoughts

Prayer Journal

Date ....

Prayers

Daily Verse & Inspiration

Praises & Gratitude

Thoughts

Prayer Journal

Date ....

Prayers

Daily Verse & Inspiration

Praises & Gratitude

Thoughts

Prayer Journal

Date ....

Prayers

Daily Verse & Inspiration

Praises & Gratitude

Thoughts

Prayer Journal

Date ....

Prayers

Daily Verse & Inspiration

Praises & Gratitude

Thoughts

Prayer Journal

Date ....

Prayers

....

....

....

Daily Verse & Inspiration

Praises & Gratitude

Thoughts

Prayer Journal

Date ....

Prayers

```
Daily Verse & Inspiration
```

Praises & Gratitude

Thoughts

Prayer Journal

Date ....

Prayers

--- Daily Verse & Inspiration ---

Praises & Gratitude

Thoughts

Prayer Journal

Date _____

Prayers

Daily Verse & Inspiration

Praises & Gratitude

Thoughts

Prayer Journal

Date ....

Prayers

Daily Verse & Inspiration

Praises & Gratitude

Thoughts

Prayer Journal

Date ....

Prayers

Daily Verse & Inspiration

Praises & Gratitude

Thoughts

Prayer Journal

Date ....

Prayers

Daily Verse & Inspiration

Praises & Gratitude

Thoughts

Prayer Journal

Date _____

Prayers

Daily Verse & Inspiration

Praises & Gratitude

Thoughts

Prayer Journal

Date ....

Prayers

Daily Verse & Inspiration

Praises & Gratitude

Thoughts

Prayer Journal

Date _____

Prayers

Daily Verse & Inspiration

Praises & Gratitude

Thoughts

Prayer Journal

Date ....

Prayers

Daily Verse & Inspiration

Praises & Gratitude

Thoughts

Prayer Journal

Date ....

Prayers

Daily Verse & Inspiration

Praises & Gratitude

Thoughts

Prayer Journal

Date ....

Prayers

Daily Verse & Inspiration

Praises & Gratitude

Thoughts

Prayer Journal

Date ....

Prayers

Daily Verse & Inspiration

Praises & Gratitude

Thoughts

Prayer Journal

Date ....

Prayers

Daily Verse & Inspiration

Praises & Gratitude

Thoughts

Prayer Journal

Date ....

Prayers

Daily Verse & Inspiration

Praises & Gratitude

Thoughts

Prayer Journal

Date ....

Prayers

Daily Verse & Inspiration

Praises & Gratitude

Thoughts

Prayer Journal

Date ....

Prayers

Daily Verse & Inspiration

Praises & Gratitude

Thoughts

Prayer Journal

Date ....

Prayers

Daily Verse & Inspiration

Praises & Gratitude

Thoughts

Prayer Journal

Date _____

Prayers

_____

_____

_____

_____

_____

_____

_____

Daily Verse & Inspiration

Praises & Gratitude

_____

_____

_____

Thoughts

Prayer Journal

Date ....

 *Prayers*

Daily Verse & Inspiration

Praises & Gratitude

Thoughts

Prayer Journal

Date _____

Prayers

Daily Verse & Inspiration

Praises & Gratitude

Thoughts

Prayer Journal

Date ....

Prayers

....

....

....

Daily Verse & Inspiration

Praises & Gratitude

Thoughts

Prayer Journal

Date ....

Prayers

Daily Verse & Inspiration

Praises & Gratitude

Thoughts

Prayer Journal

Date ....

Prayers

Daily Verse & Inspiration

Praises & Gratitude

Thoughts

Prayer Journal

Date _____

Prayers

Daily Verse & Inspiration

Praises & Gratitude

Thoughts

Prayer Journal

Date ....

Prayers

Daily Verse & Inspiration

Praises & Gratitude

Thoughts

Prayer Journal

Date _____

Prayers

Daily Verse & Inspiration

Praises & Gratitude

Thoughts

Prayer Journal

Date ....

Prayers

Daily Verse & Inspiration

Praises & Gratitude

Thoughts

Prayer Journal

Date

Prayers

Daily Verse & Inspiration

Praises & Gratitude

Thoughts

Prayer Journal

Date

Prayers

Daily Verse & Inspiration

Praises & Gratitude

Thoughts

Wrapping it up!

Self care is extremely important. You can be more effective and you can become more connected with yourself when you practice good self-care. You will be able to handle stress better and you can become more productive in your day and in your relationships. These are just a few of the benefits of effective self care. It is important to re-evaluation your self care levels and needs throughout your life, and make appropriate adjustments in particular if there are life changes and/or challenges.

You can do this.
You deserve this!
Self care is not selfish!